Oxford Read and Discover

All About Islands
Activity Book

Name: _____

Age: _____

Class: _____

School: _____

OXFORD
UNIVERSITY PRESS

Great Clarendon Street, Oxford OX2 6DP

Oxford University Press is a department of the University of Oxford.
It furthers the University's objective of excellence in research, scholarship,
and education by publishing worldwide in

Oxford New York

Auckland Cape Town Dar es Salaam Hong Kong Karachi
Kuala Lumpur Madrid Melbourne Mexico City Nairobi
New Delhi Shanghai Taipei Toronto

With offices in

Argentina Austria Brazil Chile Czech Republic France Greece
Guatemala Hungary Italy Japan Poland Portugal Singapore
South Korea Switzerland Thailand Turkey Ukraine Vietnam

OXFORD and OXFORD ENGLISH are registered trade marks of
Oxford University Press in the UK and in certain other countries

© Oxford University Press 2011

The moral rights of the author have been asserted

Database right Oxford University Press (maker)

First published 2011
2017
10 9 8 7 6 5 4 3

No unauthorized photocopying

All rights reserved. No part of this publication may be reproduced,
stored in a retrieval system, or transmitted, in any form or by any means,
without the prior permission in writing of Oxford University Press,
or as expressly permitted by law, or under terms agreed with the appropriate
reprographics rights organization. Enquiries concerning reproduction outside
the scope of the above should be sent to the ELT Rights Department, Oxford
University Press, at the address above

You must not circulate this book in any other binding or cover
and you must impose this same condition on any acquirer

Any websites referred to in this publication are in the public domain and
their addresses are provided by Oxford University Press for information only.
Oxford University Press disclaims any responsibility for the content

ISBN: 978 0 19 464513 3

Printed in China

This book is printed on paper from certified and well-managed sources.

ACKNOWLEDGEMENTS

All About Islands Activity Book by: Alistair McCallum
Illustrations by: Kelly Kennedy, Alan Rowe, Mark Ruffle, and Jane Smith

Introduction  Page 3

1 Circle the correct words.

1 About **50%** / **10%** / **90%** of people in the world live on islands.
2 An island is a piece of land with **water** / **sand** / **trees** all around it.
3 **All** / **Most** / **Some** islands are very small.
4 There's a volcano on **Manhattan** / **Honshu** / **Hong Kong** island.
5 Some islands in **hot** / **cold** / **warm** places are covered with ice.
6 Some big islands, like **Iceland** / **Hawaii** / **Manhattan**, are countries.

2 Answer the questions.

1 Are there any islands in your country?
   _____

2 Do you live on an island?
   _____

3 What islands have you visited?
   _____

4 Write the names of two big islands, and two small islands.
   _____
   _____

5 Have you ever seen a volcano? Was it on an island?
   _____

 **What Is an Island?**

1 Write the words.

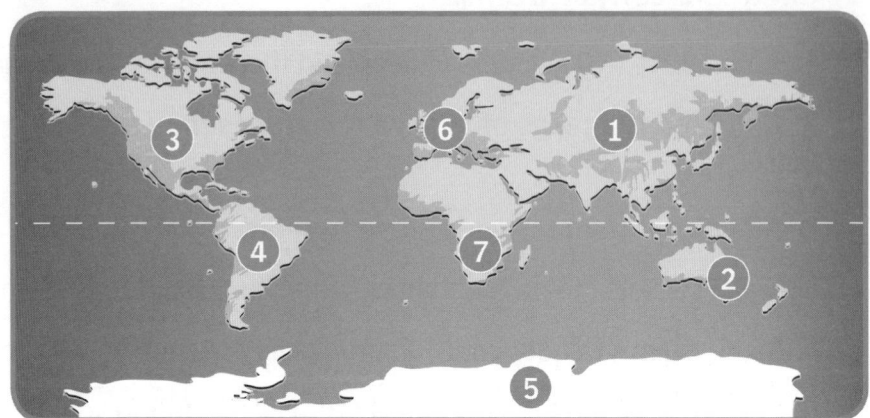

1 A _sia_
2 A _____
3 N _____ A _____
4 S _____ A _____
5 A _____
6 E _____
7 A _____

2 Complete the sentences.

1 Islands can _f_ _o_ _r_ _m_ in a lot of different ways.

2 About 20,000 years ago, lots of water from the oceans _ _ _ _ _ into ice, and the sea _ _ _ _ _ went down everywhere.

3 Later, Earth became warmer and a lot of the ice _ _ _ _ _ _ _.

4 Volcanoes under the ocean _ _ _ _ _ and the _ _ _ _ _ can form volcanic islands.

3 Correct the sentences.

1 More than 30% of Earth's surface is land.
   Less than 30% of Earth's surface is land.

2 An island is a piece of land with mountains all around it.
   _____

3 There are five continents and thousands of islands.
   _____

4 About 20,000 years ago, Earth was very warm.
   _____

5 In 2009, a new volcanic island formed in the Atlantic Ocean, near Tonga.
   _____

4 Complete the sentences.

> dinosaurs teeth poison ~~species~~ million
> nose mainland insects mammal

1 The animals and plants on some islands grow in different ways from the _species_ on the _____.

2 Solenodons have a long _____ and they are the only _____ with _____ in their teeth.

3 They use their nose and _____ to hunt _____ and other small animals.

4 They lived at the time of the _____, 65 _____ years ago.

2 Volcanic Islands (← Pages 8–11)

1 Match. Then write sentences.

When a volcano erupts,	getting bigger every year.
The volcano on Stromboli	have black beaches.
Some of the Canary Islands	lava flies into the air.
Mount Fuji hasn't erupted	are active volcanoes.
Hawaii is	erupts about every two hours.
Stromboli and Mount Fuji	for more than 300 years.

1 When a volcano erupts, lava flies into the air.
2 _____
3 _____
4 _____
5 _____
6 _____

2 Complete the sentences.

> pools   island   eggs   steam   winter   boils   ash   geysers

1 When water meets hot volcanic rock, the water _____.
  Some of the hot water evaporates into _____.

2 Iceland is a volcanic _____ with a lot of _____.

3 Iceland is cold, but even in _____, there are hot water _____ where people can swim.

4 Some birds on volcanic islands leave their _____ in warm volcanic _____.

3 Number the sentences in order (1 = first, 6 = last).

1 Plants grow, because the rock contains minerals. ☐

2 The lava cools and forms rock. ☐

3 When the plants die, they form soil and then more plants grow. ☐

4 A volcano erupts. ☐ 1

5 After thousands of years, big forests grow. ☐

6 Birds drop plants and seeds onto the rock when they are flying over. ☐

4 Order the words.

1 islands / Indonesia. / 17,500 / about / in / are / There
   There are about 17,500 islands in Indonesia.

2 flower / Rafflesia arnoldii. / world's / The / is / biggest / the
   _____

3 smells / Rafflesia arnoldii / horrible. / The
   _____

4 trees / on / are / big / There / Sumatra. / very
   _____

5 and more / year / trees. / down / people / Every / more / cut
   _____

6 trees / the forests. / will / no more / there / One day, / big / be / in
   _____

3 Tropical Islands ← Pages 12–15

1 Write the words.

1 c _oconut_   2 s _____   3 s _____
                                t _____

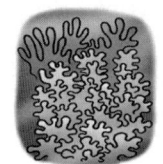

4 c _____   5 j _____   6 c _____

2 Match. Then write sentences.

Coral	make	in large groups.
Coconut crabs	looks	on the island of Mauritius.
The dodo	fly	very strong.
Corals	are	away from danger.
People	lived	like a colorful plant.
Birds	grow	houses from bamboo.

1 _____
2 _____
3 _____
4 _____
5 _____
6 _____

3 Order the words. Then answer the questions.

1 Great / is / Reef? / the / Where / Barrier
   Where is the Great Barrier Reef?
   It's near Australia.

2 box jellyfish / hard / see? / are / Why / to
   _____
   _____

3 islands / many / the / How / there / are / Pacific Ocean? / in
   _____
   _____

4 the / did / last / die? / dodo / When
   _____
   _____

4 Complete the sentences.

1 When corals d<u>ie</u>_____, they produce hard s_____.
2 Box jellyfish are some of the most p_____ animals on Earth, and you should never t_____ them.
3 The coconut c_____ is very strong, and it can open a coconut with its l_____.
4 On Pentecost Island, men climb up bamboo towers, then they d_____ toward the ground with ropes around their a_____.

4 Amazing Island Species 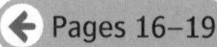 Pages 16–19

1 Write the words.

> tortoise   tree   ~~dragon~~   Galapagos   lemur   kangaroo
> rat   ~~Komodo~~   spider   woolly   jumping

1 <u>Komodo dragon</u>   2 _____   3 _____

4 _____   5 _____   6 _____

2 Order the words. Then write *true* or *false*.

1 run / dragon / can / Komodo / fast. / The
   <u>The Komodo dragon can run fast.</u>   <u>true</u>

2 animals / scared / Most / people. / are / of / wild
   _____   _____

3 lizard / smallest / Earth. / dragon / the / Komodo / is / The / on
   _____   _____

4 dragons / trees. / Young / live / Komodo / in
   _____   _____

5 long / communicate / its / A lemur / tail / with people. / to / uses
   _____   _____

3 Correct the sentences.

1 Madagascar is a big island in the Pacific Ocean.
_____

2 The Komodo dragon has poison in its tail.
_____

3 On New Guinea, there are kangaroos that live in lakes.
_____

4 Baobab trees can live for 100 years.
_____

5 Lemurs only live on the Galapagos Islands.
_____

6 A lemur uses its feet to communicate with other lemurs.
_____

4 Complete the paragraph.

> trees   rainy   ground   differences   grass   islands
> neck   short

There are important _____ between the tortoises on the different Galapagos islands. Some of the _____ are dry, and some are _____. The tortoises on the dry islands have a long _____. This helps them to eat the leaves of _____. The tortoises on the rainy islands have a _____ neck because they eat _____ and other plants on the _____.

5 Remote Islands ← Pages 20–23

1 Write the words. Then match with the definitions.

1 esnkas snakes   5 sbalarosset _____
2 inpensgu _____   6 ayaspap _____
3 sabanna _____   7 dalzris _____
4 noelechams _____   8 ostuconc _____

a These animals live on Socotra: _1_, ____, ____

b These fruits grow on Anuta: ____, ____, ____

c These birds live on Tristan da Cunha: ____, ____

2 Match. Then write sentences.

Anuta is a remote island	can change color.
The winds are strong	made big statues.
Once, Easter Island	in the Pacific Ocean.
People on Easter Island	on Tristan da Cunha.
Some chameleons	in two different places.
A chameleon's eyes can look	had big forests.

1 _____
2 _____
3 _____
4 _____
5 _____
6 _____

3 Order the words. Then answer the questions.

1 hot / Is / on / the / Anuta? / weather

   Is the weather hot on Anuta?

   Yes, it is.

2 use / Anuta? / money / on / they / Do

   _____

   _____

3 English / Tristan da Cunha? / people / Do / on / speak

   _____

   _____

4 there / trees / lot / Are / on / a / Easter Island? / of

   _____

   _____

4 Complete the sentences.

1 Anuta is not big. It's _ _ _ _. Sometimes the people grow food in a _ _ _ _ _ _ on another island.

2 Easter Island is 3,500 kilometers from Chile. It's _ _ _ _ _ _ _.

3 The statues on Easter Island are made of _ _ _ _ _ _ _ _ _ rock.

4 The Ancient Romans used the _ _ _ _ _ of the dragon's blood tree as a _ _ _ _ _ _ _ _.

6 Big Islands Pages 24–27

1 Circle the correct answers.

1 ___ is a country.
   a Baffin Island   **b Madagascar**   c North Island

2 The biggest islands are all ___.
   a in the Pacific Ocean   b near a continent   c near the equator

3 The biggest island in the world is ___.
   a New Guinea   b Easter Island   c Greenland

4 Lots of people live on ___.
   a Greenland   b Honshu   c New Guinea

5 ___ is part of Canada.
   a Baffin Island   b Greenland   c Tasmania

6 Most of the people on ___ are Inuit.
   a Tasmania   b Madagascar   c Greenland

2 Write Greenland, Tasmania, or New Zealand.

1 The Lord of the Rings movies were filmed here. _New Zealand_
2 Polar bears live here. _____
3 There are two big islands in this country. _____
4 This is a big island south of Australia. _____
5 It's three times bigger than any other island. _____
6 The heaviest insect in the world lives here. _____
7 It's mostly white with ice and snow. _____

3 Write the words. Then answer the questions.

> How many   What   Why   How much   ~~Which~~   What

1 _Which_ is the biggest island in the world?
   Greenland is the biggest island in the world.

2 _____ do many Inuit people hunt?
   _____

3 _____ people live on Greenland?
   _____

4 _____ color is the Arctic fox?
   _____

5 _____ meat can a Tasmanian devil eat?
   _____

6 _____ can polar bears walk easily on the snow?
   _____

4 Complete the sentences.

1 The biggest islands are all near a _ _ _ _ _ _ _ _ _.
2 Polar bears have black _ _ _ _ and white _ _ _.
3 The kiwi is a _ _ _ _ that can't _ _ _.
4 The weta is the _ _ _ _ _ _ _ _ insect on Earth.
5 When the Tasmanian devil is _ _ _ _ _ _, it makes a horrible _ _ _ _ _.

7 Man-Made Islands ← Pages 28–31

1 Match. Then write sentences.

Sometimes people build cities
The Intha people's houses are
Intha men use their legs
Tourists in Dubai like
Incheon is one of

to row their boats.
on man-made islands.
the busiest airports in the world.
the clear blue ocean.
on wooden stilts.

1 _____
2 _____
3 _____
4 _____
5 _____

2 Complete the sentences.

China   Dubai   Japan   Burma   South Korea   Japan

1 Odaiba Island is in Tokyo Bay in _____.

2 Inle Lake is in _____.

3 The Burj Al Arab hotel is in _____.

4 _____ has two airports that are built on man-made islands.

5 Incheon International Airport is in _____.

6 The first airport built on a man-made island was Kansai International Airport in _____.

3 Order the words. Then answer the questions.

1 people / new islands? / do / sometimes / Why / build

_____

_____

2 Odaiba Island / Why / built? / was

_____

_____

3 do / people / the / live? / Intha / Where

_____

_____

4 Intha people / What / the / their islands? / grow / on / do

_____

_____

4 Complete the sentences.

1 Today, Odaiba Island is a b_____ part of Tokyo city.
2 The Intha people make f_____ islands with reeds.
3 Reeds are a type of thick g_____.
4 The Intha people grow rice and v_____ on their islands. They also go f_____ in the lake.
5 The Burj Al Arab hotel looks like the s_____ of a boat.
6 The b_____ from Incheon airport to the mainland is more than 20 kilometers long.

8 Protecting Our Islands  Pages 32–35

1 **Write the words. Then complete the sentences.**

t_ex_tc_{in} _extinct_   a_{se} v_el_{el} _____

p_er_ad_ip_{as} _____   a_rn_cb_o e_xi_do_{di} _____

b_algol m_ani_{wgr} _____   e_yt_ic_lc_et_ir _____

1 Life on islands is often in danger, and species can become _extinct_.

2 Earth is getting warmer because there's too much _____ in the air.

3 We should use less coal and oil to make _____.

4 More ice is melting, so the _____ is getting higher.

5 _____ means that there are more storms and rain.

6 Some islands in the Pacific Ocean will probably _____ in 100 years.

2 **Complete the sentences.**

> use   visit   slow   kill   fly

1 We can try to _____ down global warming by making less carbon dioxide.

2 We can drive and _____ less.

3 We can _____ cleaner cars.

4 Storms and floods can _____ plants and animals.

5 When too many tourists _____ small islands, it's bad for plant and animal life.

3 Order the words.

1 often / islands / on / is / in danger. / Life

_____

2 make / should / less / use / coal and oil / We / electricity. / to

_____

3 changing / warming / is / Global / on / islands. / life

_____

4 can / plants and animals. / kill / and floods / Storms

_____

5 gets / seawater / Coral / when / warm. / too / dies

_____

6 around / reefs. / species / Thousands / coral / of / live

_____

4 Complete the sentences.

1 The Svalbard Islands are in the _ _ _ _ _ _ Ocean.
2 Global warming probably won't _ _ _ _ Svalbard's ice.
3 Scientists from _ _ _ _ _ _ built the Svalbard Global Seed Vault in 2008.
4 It's a place where they will _ _ _ _ _ an example of each of Earth's 1.5 million _ _ _ _ _.
5 The Global Seed Vault is inside a rocky _ _ _ _ _ _ _ _ at the end of a long _ _ _ _ _ _.
6 Most seeds will stay _ _ _ _ _ at minus 18 degrees centigrade for 20,000 years.

After Reading 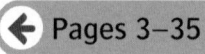 Pages 3–35

1 **Check your answers to Activity 1, page 3.**

   1 = 10%   2 = water   3 = Some
   4 = Honshu   5 = cold   6 = Iceland

2 **Complete the puzzle.**

1 There is water all around an ___.
2 There is too much ___ dioxide in the air.
3 The Tasmanian ___ has very sharp teeth.
4 People on Easter Island made big ___.
5 ___ bears have black skin and white fur.
6 ___ Island is in Tokyo Bay in Japan.
7 Global ___ is changing life on islands.
8 ___ from a volcano can form an island.
9 Millions of ___ are stored on the Svalbard Islands.
10 ___ plants grow tall and strong on tropical islands.
11 A ___ is an animal that can change color.
12 When volcanoes ___, hot gases and ash fly into the air.
13 Asia and Africa are ___.

20

3 Write the words. Then find and write the page.

1 There are about 17,500 islands in
   this country. __Indonesia__   __page 11__
2 This is the largest lizard on Earth. _____   _____
3 This volcano in the Mediterranean Sea erupts
   every two hours. _____   _____
4 The people on Tristan da Cunha speak
   this language. _____   _____
5 These small animals grow in large groups
   in tropical seawater. _____   _____
6 Earth is getting warmer because there is
   too much of this gas in the air. _____   _____
7 Scientists have found a giant jumping spider
   on this island. _____   _____
8 The statues on Easter Island are made
   of this. _____   _____
9 There are baobab trees and lemurs on
   this island. _____   _____
10 These islands are famous for
   their tortoises. _____   _____
11 This is the biggest island on Earth. _____   _____
12 This bird couldn't fly, and it became extinct
   in about 1700. _____   _____

21

4 Complete the sentences.

> away   on   into   down   around   above

1. There is water all _____ an island.
2. When volcanoes erupt, ash and lava fly _____ the air.
3. Most wild animals run _____ from people.
4. Most of the land in the Maldive Islands is less than 2 meters _____ sea level.
5. Every year people cut _____ more and more trees.
6. Polar bears have huge paws, so they can walk easily _____ the snow.

5 Match. Then write questions and answers.

Can	you touch box jellyfish?
Do	it rain every day in Madagascar?
Is	polar bears have white skin?
Should	woolly rats scared of people?
Are	Earth very cold 20,000 years ago?
Was	the Komodo dragon swim fast?
Does	Hawaii getting bigger?

1. _Can the Komodo dragon swim fast?_   _Yes, it can._
2. _____   _____
3. _____   _____
4. _____   _____
5. _____   _____
6. _____   _____
7. _____   _____

6 Complete the chart using words from A, B, and C.

A Indian Atlantic ~~Arctic~~ Pacific

B ~~biggest~~ remote 250 people plant

C airport / ships / every year
money / share / everything
30 meters / live / 1,000 years
~~green / white / ice and snow~~

Greenland	It's in the ___Artic___ Ocean. It's the ___biggest___ island in the world. It isn't _green. It's mostly white with ice and snow._
Anuta	It's in the _____ Ocean. About _____ live there. They don't _____.
Madagascar	It's in the _____ Ocean. There are 10,000 species of _____ there. Madagascar baobab trees can grow _____.
Tristan da Cunha	It's in the _____ Ocean. It's a very _____ island. There isn't _____.

 # My Book Review

Title of this book: _____

Name of the author: _____

This book is about _____ .

Questions about this book

1 What new words did you learn from this book? (Write six words.)
   _____
   _____

2 Which islands did you learn about? (Write two islands.)
   _____

3 Which animals did you learn about? (Write two animals.)
   _____

4 Which island in the book do you want to visit? Why?
   _____

What I like about this book

My favorite chapter was _____.

My favorite picture was _____.

My scores for this book (draw ☺, ☺☺, or ☺☺☺)

Interesting book ○○○   Interesting cover ○○○

Interesting pictures ○○○   Fun to read ○○○

Which book do you want to read next? _____